BRITISH RAILWAYS

PAST and PRESENT

No 53

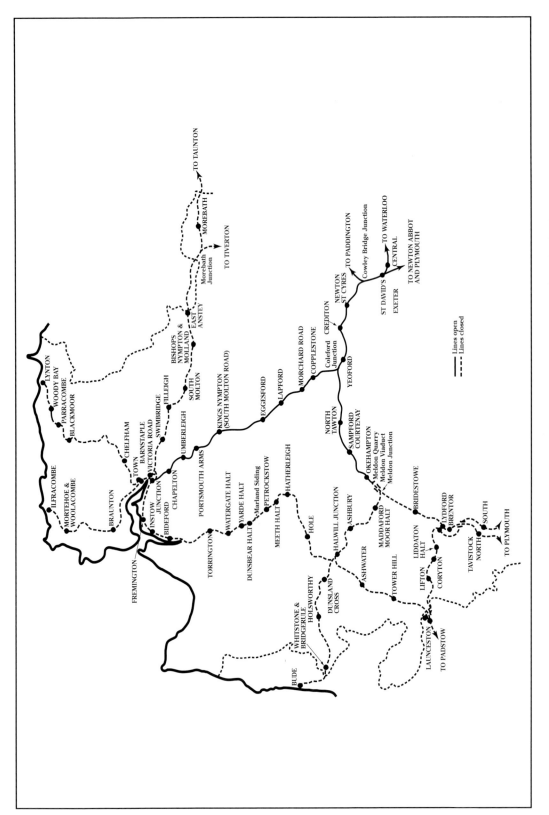

Map of the area covered by this book, showing locations featured or referred to in the text.

BRITISH RAILWAYS

PAST and PRESENT

No 53

North and West Devon

David Mitchell

Past & Present Publishing Ltd

First published in 2006
Reprinted 2008

British Library Cataloguing in Publication Data

A catalogue record for this book is available from the British Library.

ISBN 978 1 85895 245 1

Past & Present Publishing Ltd
The Trundle
Ringstead Road
Great Addington
Kettering
Northants NN14 4BW

Tel/Fax: 01536 330588
email: sales@nostalgiacollection.com
Website: www.nostalgiacollection.com

Printed and bound in the Czech Republic

BARNSTAPLE JUNCTION: Former Great Western 'Mogul' No 7337 is reversing over the middle siding on Saturday 21 March 1964, before picking up empty stock that will be drawn into the nearest platform to form the 2.20pm departure to Taunton. On the left is the down island platform, while out of view to the right of the camera is the wooden goods shed.

   The middle siding was truncated at the far end in 1971, and at about the same time the track on the far side of the island platform was also taken out of use. The other down line was retained as part of a run-round loop until 1990, but in July 2005 only a single line survives to serve the remaining platform. *Derek Frost/DHM*

CONTENTS

OKEHAMPTON: The station site was cut into the slopes of East Hill, and on its south side borders Dartmoor; it is perched high above the town, the centre of which is about half a mile down the hillside. Platform 2 was the main down platform, used by Plymouth services and through trains to Bude and North Cornwall. On 27 April 1963 'Battle of Britain' 4-6-2 No 34056 *Croydon* is working the 11.55am Exeter Central to Plymouth train, while 'N' Class 2-6-0 No 31839 waits to follow from Platform 1 with the 1.18pm departure to Bude.

The Dartmoor Railway's basic service takes the form of a shuttle between here and Meldon. FM Rail is using Meldon Quarry to store some of its surplus locomotives, and an operational duo, Brush Type 4 No 47716 and electro-diesel No 73134, head the 1600 departure on 31 August 2004. *Derek Frost/DHM*

INTRODUCTION

I n the second part of our present survey of Devonshire's railways, a look is taken at that part
of the county that was dominated by the Southern Railway, although this book is 'top-and-
tailed' by two Great Western routes. The Southern's network west of Exeter has long been
known as 'The Withered Arm', referring to the way in which the various routes penetrated
sparsely populated areas, with long spindly limbs reaching to the northern and western
extremities of the county.

Due in the main to this relatively small population, the 1960s saw the widespread closure
of most of the lines featured in this title, and today only the Barnstaple branch remains as part
of the national network. This line is operated as part of the Wessex Trains franchise, and since
1990 has been promoted as 'The Tarka Line'. Currently 12 return trains to Barnstaple are
provided each weekday, a more frequent service than in the past, and patronage has
increased – 240,000 journeys were recorded in 2004, a 21% increase over the preceding three
years. The line provides a vital link to North Devon, but is more than twice as busy in the
summer than the winter, thus proving its attraction to the leisure market. To maintain the
current level of service the DMU fleet has to be fairly intensively used, and this means that
the service to some of the little-used intermediate stations has been reduced. However, this
is justified as the vast majority of journeys are to and from Barnstaple itself, with Crediton the
only other station seeing a significant number of passengers; the 'top' journey is from
Barnstaple to Exeter Central. Interestingly, only 64% of journeys are internal to the line (ie
going no further than Central), proving that a sizeable proportion of passengers connect into
and from other parts of the network.

The passenger service to Okehampton survived until 1972, but the line was retained
thereafter to handle ballast trains from Meldon Quarry. In the later years of public ownership,
the quarry operated as a wholly owned subsidiary of British Rail, but was sold to Camas
Aggregates in 1994, together with the railway from Coleford Junction. Since privatisation, the
quarry has had a somewhat chequered history. Traditionally it supplied ballast to the
Southern Region and its predecessors, but this had ceased in 1993, leaving only a smaller
contract to satisfy West Country needs. This too ended in 1998 when Railtrack rationalised its
ballast requirements with a 'virtual quarry' established at Westbury, mainly supplied with
ballast from Scotland shipped via Southampton Docks. Despite producing a high-quality
product, Meldon suffered from both a need for investment and high transportation costs. No
trains departed the quarry for about seven months until a contract was obtained for stone
dust, used in connection with a fibre optic cable-laying contract. A series of trains ran to
various terminals until September 2000, when the contractor went into liquidation. One year
later a short-term contract was obtained to supply ballast to the national network, but there
then followed a gap of almost two years before Meldon stone was used in the scheme to re-
double the Burngullow to Probus section of railway in Cornwall. It is pleasing to report that a
further contract was obtained from Network Rail in March 2005, and at the time of writing
three or four trains are usually operating from the quarry each week.

In the meantime a limited passenger service returned to the line on summer Sundays from
May 1997, promoted by Devon County Council, West Devon Borough Council and the
Dartmoor National Park, with services operated by Wessex Trains. At the restored
Okehampton station, trains connect with buses that transport visitors to places on Dartmoor
and beyond. The quarry and railway are currently owned by Aggregate Industries, and, with
the limited number of stone trains, the Dartmoor Railway was established to make better use
of the infrastructure. From 2000 the 'Dartmoor Pony' service has operated between

Okehampton and a new station at Meldon, where visitors can walk across the restored viaduct. Services have subsequently been extended to Sampford Courtenay, and long-term plans include daily services to Exeter and the opening of a park-and-ride station on the eastern outskirts of Okehampton.

The Lynton & Barnstaple Railway served a particularly small population, and the line was an early casualty, closing in 1935. With its glorious route across the foothills of Exmoor, it would have made a wonderful tourist attraction and it is a shame that it did not survive another 10 or 15 years, when it is likely that its charms would have appealed to that early generation of preservationists who were responsible for saving the famous Welsh narrow gauge railways. However, a group are intent on rebuilding as much of the line as possible, and a visit is recommended to the foothold that they have established at the delightful Woody Bay station.

Although the railway network has greatly diminished within the area covered by this book, we are fortunate that long stretches are still available for public use in the form of the Tarka Trail and Granite Way. By walking and cycling along these routes it is still possible to enjoy some of the wonderful countryside seen by previous generations through the carriage window.

I am extremely grateful to the photographers who have provided material for this book, and to the landowners who granted me permission to enter their private property. My thanks also go to Andrew Griffiths, Business Manager for Wessex Trains, for providing certain information, and to Eric Youldon for his comments on the manuscript.

David Mitchell, Exeter

BIBLIOGRAPHY

Anthony, G. H. *The Tavistock, Launceston & Princetown Railways* (Oakwood, 1971)
Gough, Terry *The Tarka & Dartmoor Lines* (Past & Present, 1998)
    The Tarka Trail (Past & Present, 1998)
    The Tamar & Tavy Valleys (Past & Present, 2001)
Gray, Peter W. *Steam in Devon* (Ian Allan, 1995)
Maggs, C. *The Taunton to Barnstaple Line* (Oakwood)
Mitchell, David *BR Past & Present No 8 Devon* (Past & Present, 1991)
    BR Past & Present No 17 Cornwall (Past & Present, 1993)
    BR Past & Present No 30 Somerset (Past & Present, 1996)
    BR Past & Present No 52 East Devon (Past & Present, 2005)
Mitchell, Vic and Smith, Keith *Taunton to Barnstaple* (Middleton, 1995)
    Exeter to Barnstaple (Middleton, 1993)
    Branch Line to Ilfracombe (Middleton, 1993)
    Branch Lines to Torrington (Middleton, 1994)
    Exeter to Tavistock (Middleton, 1996)
    Tavistock to Plymouth (Middleton, 1996)
    Branch Line to Bude (Middleton, 1996)
    Branch Lines to Launceston and Princetown (Middleton, 1998)
Nicholas, John *Lines to Torrington* (OPC, 1984)
    The North Devon Line (OPC, 1992)
Nicholas, John and Reeve, George *The Okehampton Line* (Irwell, 2001)
Pryer, G. A. *Track Layout Diagrams of the SR Section 6* (R. A. Cooke, 1983)
Wroe, D. J. *The Bude Branch* (Kingfisher, 1988)
    North Cornwall Railway (Irwell, 1995)

Morebath Junction to Barnstaple
(Devon & Somerset Railway)

MOREBATH JUNCTION: The broad gauge Devon & Somerset Railway opened as far as Wiveliscombe in 1871, the remainder of the route from there to Barnstaple coming into use on 1 November 1873. It was initially operated by the Bristol & Exeter Railway, and by the Great Western from 1876. The junction came into being on 1 August 1884 when the line to Tiverton opened. On 7 September 1963 0-4-2T No 1450 is propelling the 1.5pm SO Dulverton to Exeter St David's auto-train past the signal box and over the junction before heading south, one month before the Exe Valley service ended.

Rather than a view of today's flora, this 'not quite so past' comparison from 3 August 1964 shows 2-6-0 No 7337 passing with the 11.25am Taunton to Barnstaple service. The signal box had closed on 29 April when the loop had been taken out of use. Both have been removed; as has the Exe Valley junction. *Both R. A. Lumber*

EAST ANSTEY: The line crosses back into Somerset a mile west of Morebath Junction, and remains in that county for about 4 miles before re-entering Devon just before reaching this village. A passing loop was provided here in 1876, and was subsequently lengthened in both 1910 and 1937. 'Mogul' No 7333 is pausing with the 1.5pm Taunton to Barnstaple train on Tuesday 2 October 1962, and is standing next to the goods shed.

Goods traffic here ceased in September 1963, and both the goods shed and main station building have been converted into houses. This and the next four 'present' pictures were taken on 8 June 2005. *R. A. Lumber/DHM*

BISHOPS NYMPTON & MOLLAND station was located in the valley of the River Yeo, with Molland (its original name) 2 miles to the north-east and the larger village of Bishops Nympton almost 3 miles to the south-west. The 1755 Barnstaple to Taunton service is leaving at 1830 on 24 September 1966, one week before the passenger service ceased; the three-car DMU is passing over a low road bridge. The 30-lever signal box replaced an earlier structure when the passing loop was lengthened in 1937, while the goods shed is to the right of the camera. The line had been dieselised in September 1964.

Both the station building and goods shed here have also been converted into dwellings, and it is still possible to stand on the up platform today. Part of the down platform has, however, been demolished. *R. A. Lumber/DHM*

SOUTH MOLTON: The line was converted to standard gauge in May 1881, and after years of financial struggle was acquired by the GWR in 1901. This market town was a mile to the south of the station, and was one of the larger places served by the line. From 1928 the down platform was signalled for working in both directions and all trains used this side unless it was necessary for two trains to cross, the down side being more convenient for the town. 2-6-0 No 7337 is departing with a Taunton to Barnstaple train at 5.39pm on 8 June 1963. The goods shed is on the right.

The Pathfields Business Park now occupies the area around the station site, with the goods shed occupied by a concrete company. The North Devon Link Road (A361) runs behind the trees and along the trackbed from here to Barnstaple. The derelict station buildings survived until their demolition in about 2003. *R. A. Lumber/DHM*

FILLEIGH: The village is almost 2 miles to the south of the line, and until 1881 the station was named Castle Hill after the nearby mansion belonging to Lord Fortescue; it was renamed to avoid confusion with a London suburban station of that name, now West Ealing. A private siding existed here until prior to 1960, serving store buildings owned by the Fortescue Estate. No 7337 is passing with the 11.58am Barnstaple Junction to Cardiff train on 27 June 1964; the 43XX Class 'Moguls' first appeared on this line in about 1925 and handled most services until dieselisation.

After closure the station building was used as a house, but was subsequently demolished to make way for the 'improved' A361. The aforementioned store buildings still stand behind the trees (centre right). *R. A. Lumber/DHM*

SWIMBRIDGE: Standard Class 3MT No 82040 arrives with the 11.25am Taunton to Barnstaple train at 1.41pm on 27 June 1964. It is 42 minutes late, partly due to having been held at Filleigh for 20 minutes while waiting for an up train.

Behind the photographer is an overbridge carrying a minor road from the nearby village. Rather than stand in the middle of the A361, the author elected to record the 2005 scene from the road bridge! *R. A. Lumber/DHM*

BARNSTAPLE SOUTH LOOP JUNCTION: The Devon & Somerset terminated at Barnstaple Victoria Road station. A connecting line to the LSWR's Barnstaple Junction opened in 1887, enabling the GW to run through trains to Ilfracombe. Such workings involved a reversal in Victoria Road, but in 1905 an east curve was provided and this gave a direct run from Taunton to Barnstaple Junction. From 1925 to 1939 this curve was usually only open in the summer months to cater for holiday traffic, but was then closed, with all trains once again reversing in Victoria Road. When the latter station closed to passengers in 1960, the east curve was re-instated and all passenger trains subsequently used Barnstaple Junction. Victoria Road was retained as a goods depot until 1970, with access provided via the original west curve. The two curves joined at South Loop Junction, and on 27 June 1964 No 7306 is climbing away from this junction with a Wolverhampton to Ilfracombe service.

A gap in the trees in July 2005 allows a glimpse of the cycleway that has been built on the formation since closure. *R. A. Lumber/DHM*

Exeter Central to Ilfracombe

EXETER CENTRAL was a hive of activity in the steam era, and a fascinating place to observe the railway going about its daily business. In this scene, timed at 10.20am on 13 July 1963, Bulleid 4-6-2 No 34036 *Westward Ho* is pictured prior to working the 10.30am departure to Waterloo. The first portion of this train, the 8.10am from Ilfracombe, has arrived behind another 'Pacific', No 34106 *Lydford*, and that loco has now been uncoupled and is about to pass over the 'scissors' crossover on its way to Exmouth Junction shed. No 34036 will then pick up these coaches and pull forward, clear of the 'scissors', to await the arrival of the Plymouth portion. In the bay platform on the left a third 'West Country', No 34003 *Plymouth*, will follow with the 10.37am stopper to Salisbury.

The station is now a pale shadow of its former self, but its position in the centre of Exeter means that it is particularly useful for both commuters and shoppers, with currently more than a million passengers using it each year. On 22 August 2005 Nos 159016/007 are arriving forming the 0920 Waterloo to Plymouth service.

Peter W. Gray/DHM

17

EXETER CENTRAL: A little further westward along the same platform (No 3), but on 20 June 1958, 'Merchant Navy' 4-6-2 No 35024 *East Asiatic Company* has backed on to the front portion of the 5.52pm departure to Waterloo. In No 4 bay platform 'M7' 0-4-4T No 30670 is on the 5.35pm to Honiton, to the right of which is the goods yard. The larger Bullied 'Pacifics' were being rebuilt at this time, No 35024 being completed by the following April. The station was previously known as Queen Street and was renamed when rebuilt in 1933.

South West Trains' Nos 159013/021 arrive with the 1010 Exeter St David's to Waterloo service on 26 August 2005. *Peter W. Gray/DHM*

EXETER CENTRAL: The eight-strong class of 'Z' 0-8-0Ts was built by the Southern Railway in 1929 for heavy yard shunting work. No A954 (later 30954) was allocated to Exmouth Junction shed from new, primarily to shunt the adjacent marshalling yard; Nos 30950/6 were also sent west in February 1956 and the former is pictured next to the 'B' signal box on 18 April of that year. It had been intended that they replace the ageing 'E1/R' tanks as bankers between St David's and Central stations, but initially the Western Region refused to accept them and they did not take over the banking duties until August 1959, by which time all of the class were at Exmouth Junction. The 35-lever 'B' box opened in September 1925 and was located at the top of the incline.

The box closed in February 1970, but is still standing. Wessex Trains' No 150243 passes forming the 0919 Paignton to Exmouth service on 10 August 2005. *J. H. Bamsey/DHM*

EXETER CENTRAL: The Queen Street bridge, which is visible in the previous photos, gives a fine view of the top of the 1 in 37 incline from St David's station. On 24 May 1952 'T9' 4-4-0 No 30710 and 2-6-0 No 31847 are hauling a 12-coach Troop Special from the Bude line. The rear of the train is just leaving St David's Tunnel. On the left are carriage sidings where engines could often be found waiting to back on to the different portions of westbound trains. Two of four wagon turntables can be noted on the goods siding on the right. Visible above the 'N' is a catch siding for runaways.

A cement terminal was established in Central goods yard in the 1960s, and on 28 September 1963 Standard 2-6-4T No 80059 is piloting 4-6-0 No 6963 *Throwley Hall* with a loaded train from Westbury cement works. Banking assistance is being provided by 'W' Class 2-6-4Ts Nos 31911 and 31914; this type replaced the 'Zs' in 1962 but were not considered to be as successful as their predecessors.

The two goods sidings were taken out of use in September 1969, and the carriage sidings suffered a similar fate five months later; much of the latter area is now used for car parking. The buildings on the right were subsequently demolished, and the land was being used commercially on 4 April 1992 as 'Cromptons' Nos 33102 and D6532 climb with the 1226 Exeter St David's to Waterloo train.

The double-headed theme is completed on 24 April 2005 as 'Skips' Nos 67018 and 67016 work the 1Z83 1233 Truro to Victoria VSOE Pullman train. Reversible running is allowed over this line since resignalling in 1984. Part of the area on the right is now occupied by housing, with further land being re-developed at this time. *R. A. Lumber/Peter W. Gray/DHM(2)*

EXETER ST DAVID'S: Another cement train is captured for posterity on 26 June 1963 as it pounds over the Bonhay Road bridge, shortly before entering the 184-yard-long St David's Tunnel. The train engine is another 'Modified Hall', No 6999 *Capel Dewi Hall*, with 'W' No 31915 providing assistance on the front.

Nothing that normally tackles this incline today is heavy enough to require any assistance. On 15 July 2005 No 159004 forms the 1530 Exeter St David's to Honiton service. Growth on the bridge exemplifies the neglected appearance of much of today's network. *Derek Frost/DHM*

EXETER ST DAVID'S: Due to their different approaches to this station, Western and Southern trains bound for the same destination would travel in opposite directions from one another. This is illustrated on 9 August 1958 as veteran 'E1/R' Class 0-6-2Ts Nos 32135 and 32124 assist a Waterloo-bound train from Platform 3 at 2.8pm; the train engine is 'Battle of Britain' 4-6-2 No 34062 *17 Squadron*. In the foreground ex-GWR 2-6-0 No 6336 waits in Platform 1 with the 11.40am Bristol to Newton Abbot relief working.

Since the station was resignalled in 1985 as part of the Exeter MAS scheme, up Waterloo trains now normally use Platform 1, with down trains using either Nos 1 or 3. No 67024 is arriving with the 0728 Salisbury Yard to Riverside track recording train on 6 July 2005. *Peter W. Gray/DHM*

EXETER ST DAVID'S station dates from 1844 when the Bristol & Exeter reached the city. The LSWR's line from Queen Street station was opened in 1862, and work started at that time on rebuilding St David's to enable it to cope with the additional traffic; further reconstruction took place in 1911-14. '700' Class 0-6-0 No 30317, 'U' 2-6-0 No 31610 and 'BB' 4-6-2 No 34060 *25 Squadron* wait in Platform 3 on 9 August 1958 before departing with the 11.35am Plymouth Friary to Waterloo train. The Southern's up freights would normally use the centre road.

The latter was removed as part of the 1985 changes, while Platform 1 was also regularly used by mail trains until this business was lost to the railway in early 2004. No 67009 is heading the 1C84 2154 Reading to Plymouth train on the night of 23 December 2003. *Peter W. Gray/DHM*

EXETER ST DAVID'S: Down Southern trains used Platform 4. On 24 May 1952 4-4-0 No 30717 and ex-GWR 2-6-0 No 6301 pause with the 11.45am Exeter Central to Plymouth train; the 'T9' will be removed at Okehampton and used on a Bude service. The distinctive masonry towers house the electrically operated lifts provided in 1914 to transfer luggage between platforms.

This platform is now the usual home for westbound trains originating from Paddington or the north. On 1 September 2005 Virgin 'Voyager' No 221115 has arrived as the 0705 Leeds to Plymouth service, whilst FGW's 'Adelante' No 180109 waits in Platform 6 forming the 1156 departure to Paddington. *R. A. Lumber/DHM*

EXETER ST DAVID'S: 'T9' No 30717 features again as it passes over Red Cow level crossing on the approach to Platform 3 at 4.25pm on 9 August 1958. On its left an 'E1/R' Class tank waits in a spur used to hold banking engines. The distinctive Middle box controlled the crossing and movements at the east end of the station.

The signal box closed on 30 March 1985. Modern signalling, which is controlled from Exeter's power box, is prominent as Brush Type 4 No 47851 *Traction Magazine* passes Platform 4 with Saltburn Railtours' 1Z63 0942 Saltburn to St Austell charter train on 1 July 2005. *Peter W. Gray/DHM*

EXETER RIVERSIDE YARD dates from 1943, when extra capacity was required to deal with heavy wartime traffic. Primarily a marshalling yard, used for sorting wagons bound for various destinations, it has also been used for loading freight, such as timber. 'Peak' No 45029 is shunting its 6C43 1445 St Blazey to Severn Tunnel Junction air-braked service on 21 June 1984, mainly comprising Cornish china clay traffic. On the right are original yard buildings.

The yard has also had an important role in handling departmental traffic, but this has greatly diminished in recent years. On 1 March 2002 Nos 37042 and 37375 have run round the 6G99 Meldon Quarry to Westbury ballast train. The buildings were replaced by a Portacabin, but that too had been removed by this time. *Both DHM*

EXETER RIVERSIDE YARD: Ivatt 2-6-2T No 41322 is approaching Cowley Bridge Junction with the 5.50pm Exeter Central to Okehampton train on 8 April 1964. Just prior to this, 4-6-0 No 4088 *Dartmouth Castle* had come up to the junction as a light engine, then backed on to a freight that was standing on Riverside yard's up departure line; it is now waiting for the road. Immediately behind it is a 'Western' Class diesel-hydraulic with another up freight.

The exact viewpoint today is totally obscured by undergrowth, so No 47805 is seen closer to the junction on 10 July 2000 with the 0838 Penzance to Manchester train. No 66236 waits to follow it with the 6O92 1016 Riverside to Dollands Moor train, consisting of china clay bound for Italy. *Derek Frost/DHM*

COWLEY BRIDGE JUNCTION was created when the broad gauge Exeter & Crediton Railway opened on 12 May 1851. 'N' Class 2-6-0 No 31875 joins the Western Region's main line with a ballast train, probably the 11.35am Meldon Quarry to Exmouth Junction, at 12.56pm on 12 March 1963. It has just crossed the River Exe by way of several bridges and culverts, including the 88-yard-long viaduct visible above the engine.

In an attempt to alleviate flooding problems, the river was diverted, the bridges rebuilt and the line singled over both them and the junction; with the new layout coming into use in January 1967. The signal box closed on 30 March 1985. On 20 April 2005 EWS's No 66153 is heading the 0906 Meldon Quarry to Westbury ballast train; Freightliner took over this work in the following week. *Derek Frost/DHM*

COWLEY BRIDGE JUNCTION: Sustained and heavy rainfall in October 1960 led to the Exe and its tributary, the River Creedy, bursting their banks, causing extensive flooding to the lower-lying parts of Exeter. The railway was closed here, as pictured on the 10th, and passengers for the former Southern lines were conveyed by Devon General buses between Exeter and Crediton. Normal services resumed two days later.

Flood prevention work did not cure the potential problems here, however. On 30 October 2000 the culvert under the line and to the left of the Cowley Bridge Inn could not cope with the volume of water in the field behind the Inn. The track formation was initially undermined, then flooded by the rising torrent. The line was closed for two weeks, but more flooding on 8 December damaged the repaired track and led to a further period of closure. *Derek Frost/DHM*

PYNES: The Exeter & Crediton Railway was originally leased to the Bristol & Exeter, but from 1862 the lease was transferred to the LSWR and mixed-gauge operations were soon introduced. The line was doubled in 1875 and the LSWR had its own Cowley Bridge signal box, located on the up side of the line and just 24 chains from the GWR's box; it was closed as an economy measure in 1916. Less than half a mile from Cowley Bridge Junction the railway passes under a masonry bridge that carries a minor road from the village of Cowley to Upton Pyne. No 34086 *219 Squadron* approaches with the 11.30am Brighton to Plymouth train on 26 June 1964.

GBRf locos Nos 66708 and 73204 provide a unique sight here on 3 January 2005 as they haul the 0825 Tonbridge West to Meldon Quarry train, comprising 'Thumper' DEMUs Nos 205032/028 bound for the Dartmoor Railway. *Derek Frost/DHM*

PYNES: Broad gauge goods trains continued to run to Crediton until 1892, and thereafter the GWR retained the right to operate freight trains to the town until 1903. 'T9' 4-4-0s regularly operated on this line from about 1902 until July 1961, when the last survivors were withdrawn from Exmouth Junction shed. On 5 June that year No 30709 passes under the bridge at 6.25pm with the 3.13pm Padstow to Exeter Central service, one of the last regular duties for the class.

No 150263 forms the 1457 Barnstaple to Exmouth service on 12 August 2005. *R. A. Lumber/DHM*

PYNES: Looking in the same direction, but from the bridge, ex-SECR 'N' Class 2-6-0 No 31812 is heading an up freight on 14 April 1964. These 'Moguls' were first allocated to Exmouth Junction in 1924 and were soon hauling most of the goods and many of the passenger trains west of Exeter, work they handled competently for 40 years.

The line to Crediton was singled over the weekend of 15-16 December 1984 as part of the Exeter MAS scheme. Electric token block working was introduced at Cowley Bridge Junction box as an interim measure, until replaced by track circuit block working from 1 April 1985. The cutting is now heavily overgrown, as EWS No 66088 heads the 6F95 0925 Meldon Quarry to Westbury ballast train on a miserable 29 March 2005. This was the first working of a new contract. *Derek Frost/DHM*

NEWBRIDGE CROSS: The railway now follows the River Creedy until it reaches another bridge carrying a minor road to the village of Langford. These pages feature four pictures spanning almost 50 years. In the first, 'N' Class No 31835 is just over a mile from Cowley Bridge Junction, as it approaches the junction's distant signal with an up goods at 11.5am on 3 November 1951.

On a dull and misty 11 September 1971, Class 22 diesel-hydraulic No D6334 is working the 7B66 0920 Barnstaple to Exeter Riverside freight.

Viewed from the other end of the bridge on a cold 15 December 1984, 'Peak' No 45076 is on a train of track sections recovered from Dunscombe (between Newton St Cyres and Crediton). It is running 'wrong line' on the down rails, which are being removed during the singling work.

Finally, a typical Meldon ballast train of the time sees Nos 37047 and 37244 heading the 6C12 1142 departure from the quarry to Westbury on 15 May 1997. *Derek Frost/R. A. Lumber/ DHM(2)*

NEWTON ST CYRES station is actually located in the hamlet of Sweetham, almost a mile north of its namesake village. When the line was doubled in 1875, a signal box was provided at the Exeter end of the up platform, but this closed as an economy measure in 1930 and the frame was transferred to the station building. No footbridge was provided here and passengers were expected to use the road bridge, from which this November 1967 scene of a departing Exeter to Plymouth DMU was taken. On the right is the site of the single-siding goods yard, which had closed in 1960.

The booking office/'new' signal box closed in July 1968. The station is now a request stop and only four services in each direction are eligible to call on weekdays. On 22 November 2004 Fragonset's No 31106 passes with the 5Z31 1000 Bristol Temple Meads to Okehampton train, comprising stock bound for storage at Meldon. *R. A. Lumber/DHM*

NEWTON ST CYRES: 'N' Class 2-6-0 No 31836 approaches with the 6.00am Class 9 freight from Barnstaple Junction to Exmouth Junction on 23 August 1963. This train was due to pass here at about 10.30am, thus illustrating its leisurely progress at a maximum speed of 35mph and with stops scheduled at Umberleigh, Kings Nympton, Eggesford, Yeoford and Crediton en route. The wide separation of the tracks is a legacy of the line's broad gauge origins.

With the passage of time it is becoming harder to believe that the line was once double-track here. Freightliner's No 66516 passes between the trees with the 6F95 1030 Meldon to Hinksey Yard (Oxford) ballast train on 12 May 2005. *Peter W. Gray/DHM*

CREDITON: Bulleid 4-6-2 No 34023 *Blackmore Vale* is pictured from the down goods yard on Saturday 29 February 1964 as it departs with the 3.00pm Ilfracombe to Waterloo train, having just added some milk tanks to its load. Milk had once been forwarded from here in churns, but by the 1950s pipework had been installed for the loading of bulk milk tank wagons. Standard 4MT 2-6-4T No 80059 is standing next to the 5-ton crane in the up goods yard. The train will shortly pass the former East signal box; this had closed in 1913, but due to the length of the station layout it was retained with a ground frame to operate some of the points.

No 80059 is seen again in the second photograph, standing next to the erstwhile East box. The large building behind had originally been a cider store and slaughterhouse, but by this date was probably being used by Shippam's, the meat paste company.

The up yard remained in use for coal traffic until 4 December 1967, but from that date this business was handled at the new Exmouth Junction Coal Concentration depot. The yard was formally taken out of use and the ground frame closed in 1970, with the site subsequently taken over by Shippam's. 'Tractors' Nos 37375 and 37042 are accelerating the 1300-tonne 6G99 1042 Meldon to Westbury ballast train on 27 February 2002. *Derek Frost(2)/DHM*

CREDITON: On page 30 it was mentioned that due to the flooding on 10 October 1960, a connecting bus service was being provided between Exeter and here. In the first two photographs, taken from the east end of the down platform on that day, 'N' No 31843 is drawing its empty stock out of the down goods yard, before working to Plymouth with passengers off the 9.00am Waterloo train. On its left, 'West Country' 'Pacific' No 34096 *Trevone* will follow with a service to Ilfracombe. The main (up) goods yard is on the left, with its unusual corrugated iron shed visible.

The two sidings on the down side have been retained for the civil engineers. On a dismal 18 March 2004 Fragonset 'Cromptons' Nos 33202 and 33103 approach with the 5Z59 1016 Westbury to Okehampton train, consisting of Mark 2 stock bound for storage at Meldon Quarry.

The down sidings saw further revenue traffic from April 1999 to February 2000 when a terminal was established to receive stone dust from Meldon Quarry for use in a fibre optic cable-laying contract. Although there is a passing loop here, the current signalling arrangements meant that these trains had to run through the station and go on to Exeter Riverside to run round! On 27 May 1999 No 37521 *English China Clays* stands on the heavily overgrown track while the 6C81 1210 train from Meldon is unloaded. *Derek Frost (2)/DHM (2)*

CREDITON: In another scene from Monday 10 October 1960, 'Battle of Britain' 'Pacific' No 34080 *74 Squadron* is passing West box with the terminating 11.46am from Plymouth – the passengers will be bussed to Exeter Central for the 2.30pm departure to Waterloo. Both signal boxes were opened in 1875, with West retained after East closed in an economy measure.

West box survives today, complete with a panel installed in 1984. It acts as a 'fringe' box to the Exeter Signalling Centre at St David's and controls the routes to Barnstaple and Okehampton. On 7 September 2005 the signalman receives the single-line token from the crew on board No 66524, which is working the 6F95 1030 Meldon to Hinksey Yard ballast train. *Derek Frost/DHM*

YEOFORD: The broad gauge North Devon Railway opened from Crediton to Barnstaple in August 1854. It was leased to the LSWR in 1863 and mixed-gauge operations were soon introduced. Despite only serving a small village, Yeoford became an important interchange for both passengers and goods in 1865 with the opening of the line from Coleford Junction to North Tawton (and subsequently Plymouth and other points west). It was particularly busy with the marshalling of freight trains running to and from the two lines. Apart from the main lines, all track was taken out of use here in 1968, and the station has a woebegone look on 30 October 1976 as Nos D1009 *Western Invader* and D1023 *Western Fusilier* head the 'Westerns South Western' railtour, the 0820 from Paddington to Meldon Quarry.

Steam returned to the line on 4 October 2003 – No 34067 *Tangmere* is tailing 'Tractor' No 37308 on the returning 1528 Okehampton to Exeter St David's 'Atlantic Coast Express' charter. *R. A. Lumber/DHM*

YEOFORD: A happier scene on 20 June 1964 sees another 'Battle of Britain', No 34062 *17 Squadron*, approaching with the Okehampton to Surbiton Car Carrier, an early 'Motorail' service that operated from 1960 to 1964. These and the previous photos were taken from a road bridge that straddles the station; just out of sight to the left is a tall signal box that allowed the signalman a view over this bridge.

Since 17 October 1971 the two tracks have operated as separate routes from Crediton before diverging at the site of Coleford Junction, a mile to the west of here. On 15 March 2003 D1015 *Western Champion* returns from Okehampton with the 'Western Quarryman' railtour to Crewe. *Peter W. Gray/DHM*

COPPLESTONE: At 350 feet above sea level, this station is at the summit of the route. The line from Coleford Junction was doubled to here in November 1883, but then remained single as far as Umberleigh. Ex-GWR 2251 Class 0-6-0 No 3205 is working a short Barnstaple Junction to Exmouth Junction freight on a dreary 21 March 1964. The van is hiding the typical LSWR signal box, while the goods yard is just out of view to the left, beyond the water crane.

This is currently a request stop, but most weekday services are eligible to call. Fewer Saturday trains stop, however, including the 1224 Exmouth to Barnstaple service; No 150219 speeds by on 25 June 2005. *Derek Frost/DHM*

COPPLESTONE: The signalman has left his box, which is behind the camera, so that he can hand the single-line token to the crew aboard 'Hymek' Class 35 diesel-hydraulic No D7020. It is working the 1600 Exeter St David's to Ilfracombe train on Saturday 4 July 1970, just three months before services to that destination ceased. A water tank is visible at the end of the up platform; when such facilities were removed from South Molton Road in Southern Railway days, this was the first station after Barnstaple where up trains could take water.

The signal box closed in 1971 when the line was singled. The attractive North Devon Railway station house is now occupied privately. *R. A. Lumber/DHM*

MORCHARD ROAD: The name refers to Morchard Bishop, some 2 miles to the north-east; a road leading there crosses the railway via an attractive three-arch masonry bridge. Bulleid 4-6-2 No 34065 *Hurricane* is pictured approaching this bridge with the 9.00am Waterloo to Barnstaple Junction at 2.5pm on 5 August 1963. The rails on the right are part of the long down siding that once served a slaughterhouse loading dock. The station loop was quite short, so the passing of long trains would involve reversal into this siding.

The approach to the station is now typically overgrown. No 150251 forms the 1505 Exmouth to Umberleigh service on 17 July 2005. Passengers to Barnstaple will have to transfer to a bus due to engineering work on the north end of the line. *Peter W. Gray/DHM*

MORCHARD ROAD: In this view from the down platform, which was possibly taken in about 1960, the main station building is just visible on the left, beyond which the wooden goods shed can be glimpsed. The up platform has a typical concrete nameboard, with part of the stone-built waiting shelter just in sight. The 1873 signal box had a 12-lever frame. There are only a few houses and a hotel in the immediate vicinity and passenger traffic at this rural location has always been light, a situation not helped by the main A377 road running alongside the station.

The sidings were taken out of use at the end of February 1964, and the signal box closed one week later when the passing loop was closed. The up platform was subsequently demolished. This is currently another request stop with about a half of weekday services able to call. Single units Nos 153355/380 pass forming the 1516 Umberleigh to Exmouth service on Sunday 17 July 2005. *E. S. Youldon collection/DHM*

LAPFORD station was unusual in that the up and down platforms were staggered, with a three-arch stone bridge carrying the A377 road between them at an acute angle. The LSWR added the down platform in 1873 and this layout was the result of there being no room opposite the original 1854, and now up, platform. Access to the 'new' platform was made either by steps from the road bridge or via a boarded crossing from the up side. No 34023 *Blackmore Vale* passes the down platform as it leaves with the 12.15pm Ilfracombe to Waterloo train on 5 August 1963.

The down platform was taken out of use in about 1970, and was demolished in the early 1980s. No 66057 is hauling the 6W11 0917 Westbury to Eggesford ballast train in connection with the aforementioned engineering work on 17 July 2005. *Peter W. Gray/DHM*

LAPFORD: Looking in the other direction from the road bridge on the same day, *Blackmore Vale* enters the up platform with the same train. It is passing the 1873 built signal box, which controlled most of the station area from its 13-lever frame; there was also a ground frame at the south end of the station to operate the loop points. Out of view to the left is the Ambrosia factory; constructed in 1927, it started production of dried milk in April 1928. Other products later included tinned and clotted cream, and butter. Liquid milk for the London market was forwarded from the 1940s with the introduction of glass-lined tank wagons.

The signal box closed in June 1970, with the points at the north end also now controlled from a ground frame. General goods traffic had ended in 1967, and the creamery also closed in 1970. Its buildings were converted to other commercial use, including that of a fertiliser distribution depot, which was supplied by a weekly (as required) train. On 6 April 1992 'Tractor' No 37038 has pulled empty wagons out of the siding on the left, and is running round before taking them back to Exeter Riverside. In the 1980s the sidings were also used for grain and timber traffic.

The fertiliser traffic ended in April 1993, and the former milk factory is now mainly occupied by a furniture removal and storage company. In another 17 July 2005 view a pair of single units, Nos 153355 and 153380, pass with the 1116 Umberleigh to Exmouth service. *Peter W. Gray/DHM (2)*

Above EGGESFORD: The north end of the station is pictured from the down platform at 19.03 on Saturday 27 May 1967 with a nine-car DMU arriving as the 17.40 Exeter Central to Ilfracombe service. The goods shed is just visible on the left, but the yard here had been closed in January 1965. The 1873-built signal box is on the right, perched above a mill leat that had been channelled from the River Taw; the front is supported by the platform, with the rear on two cast iron posts. *R. A. Lumber*

Below and opposite EGGESFORD: Flooding on 21 November 1967 swept away much of the down platform, and the signal box could then only be accessed through a window! The box was closed, and the down loop was out of action for almost two years. The damage can be noted on 25 May 1968, looking north as the 1810 Ilfracombe to Exeter St David's DMU calls. Space for a new signal box has been pegged out in the foreground.

The replacement box was erected during the summer of 1969, and opened on 28 September that year; it had previously stood at Ashington Junction, near High Wycombe. It is pictured on 3 July 1982. The down platform was not restored to either its full length or width, with only a short extension added to the undamaged section.

The box closed on 1 December 1987 and train drivers now obtain tokens from cabinets at the end of each platform, while the train conductors operate the level crossing barriers. 'Hastings' DEMU No 1001 is an unusual visitor on 25 June 2005, forming the 1454 Barnstaple to Exeter St David's 'Tarka Special'. *R. A. Lumber/DHM (2)*

KING'S NYMPTON station was originally named South Molton Road, acting as a railhead for that market town even though the latter is located some 8 or 9 miles to the north. Despite the town gaining its own station with the opening of the Devon & Somerset Railway in 1873, this facility was not renamed until March 1951. The SCTS 'Exeter Flyer' railtour is returning from Torrington and Ilfracombe to Waterloo on a wet 12 September 1965, power being provided by Standard 2-6-4Ts Nos 80039 and 80043. The crossover in the foreground provides access from the down line to the small goods yard.

The yard closed in 1967 and the signal box in July 1970, when the short passing loop was taken out of use. Class 50 No D400 passes with the Barnstaple to Waterloo 'Atlantic Coast Express' charter on 18 July 1993. *R. A. Lumber/DHM*

PORTSMOUTH ARMS: This isolated station was named after the nearby inn, which had itself been named after the fourth Earl Portsmouth, who had been responsible for the construction of the turnpike road down the Taw Valley. The station acts as a railhead for a number of local villages. In this undated view, 'Battle of Britain' 'Pacific' No 34063 *229 Squadron* is passing the 10-lever 1873-built signal box as it enters with a down train. It has just passed the single-siding goods yard.

The siding was taken out of use in 1961 and the box and loop closed in 1966. This little-used request stop is, however, still open in 2005, while the former station master's house survives as a dwelling. *Author's collection/DHM*

UMBERLEIGH GATES: A signal box was established at this level crossing in October 1890. Located about a quarter of a mile south of the station, it was later reduced to a ground frame of eight levers, interlocked with Umberleigh signal box. Class 33 No 6537 is passing with the 1558 Exeter St David's to Barnstaple train on 5 October 1972. The crossing keeper lived in a railway house just visible on the left.

The ground frame closed on the following 19 November and the crossing was converted to automatic operation. The house is now occupied privately. *R. A. Lumber/DHM*

UMBERLEIGH: The 1742 Exeter Central to Ilfracombe DMU calls on Saturday 25 May 1968. The station was built on a curve and the tall down starter signal was positioned between the tracks to help visibility for engine drivers. The track was doubled from here to Pill Bridge (just south of Barnstaple) in 1890 and a new signal box was provided to accommodate the additional levers required; this can be noted beyond the waiting shelter in the centre of the up platform.

The line was singled and the signal box closed on 21 May 1971. Due to tree growth, a more head-on view on 25 June 2005 shows DEMU No 1001 again as it forms the 1326 Exeter St David's to Barnstaple service. *R. A. Lumber/DHM*

BARNSTAPLE JUNCTION: Viewed from the south end of the island platform on 21 March 1964, Ivatt 2-6-2T No 41214 is crossing over before working light engine to Torrington. It has just come from the two-road timber-built engine shed, out of view to the left. Collett 0-6-0 No 3205 will later be departing with a freight for Exeter. Behind it is the 40-lever 'A' signal box, which controlled the lines to Chapelton and Victoria Road, together with the entrance to the goods yard and engine shed.

The box closed on 1 November 1987, and now only one train is able to occupy the token section from Eggesford at any one time. The July 2005 scene shows the single track entering the former up platform. The start of a run-round loop can just be glimpsed beyond the bushes. This was laid in 1990 and is capable of taking four coaches. The remaining sidings were removed at that time. *Derek Frost/DHM*

BARNSTAPLE JUNCTION: The suffix 'Junction' was added when the Ilfracombe line opened in 1874. The 400-foot-long down platform was constructed at that time, and became an island platform (numbered 2 and 3) in 1924. In another view from that platform on 21 March 1964 we see ex-GWR 'Mogul' No 7337 standing at the original platform (No 1) before leaving with the 2.20pm departure to Taunton.

In today's 'rationalised' scene No 150230 is pictured leaving as the 1708 service to Exmouth on 10 July 2005. *Derek Frost/DHM*

BARNSTAPLE JUNCTION: In a scene from the adjacent A39 road bridge recorded on Saturday 21 March 1964, Churchward 2-6-0 No 6326 has uncoupled from its train after terminating with the 11.15am service from Taunton. Ivatt 2-6-2T No 41216 is now drawing this stock forward from Platform 3. In the foreground is the signalman's boarded crossing leading to the tablet carrier for the Torrington line.

Shortly afterwards, the Prairie tank is seen reversing the stock into Platform 2 before forming the 1.10pm departure to Torrington. Just visible on the left is the 'B' signal box, which controlled the lines to Torrington and Ilfracombe; the latter route is curving away on the far side of the box. The goods yard can be noted in the left distance. The main station building was the work of architect Sir William Tite, and the covered footbridge dated from 1878, with a 1924 extension over the 'new' Platform 3 road.

The Ilfracombe line closed in October 1970, and the signal box was taken out of use in May 1971. The Torrington route finally closed in 1982, but a portion beyond the bridge was kept as part of a run-round loop. In the third photograph an HST set (power cars Nos 43099 and 43076) is an unusual visitor with the 0817 charter from Paddington on 18 March 1990. The tour had earlier visited Meldon Quarry.

The loop was taken out of use in the following August when the aforementioned shorter one was provided. In July 2005 a rough access track had been created in the right foreground in connection with new road works.
Derek Frost (2)/DHM (2)

BARNSTAPLE TOWN: The Barnstaple & Ilfracombe Railway opened on 20 July 1874 and the LSWR operated it from the outset, absorbing the company in 1875. Barnstaple Quay station was located at the northern end of a bridge over the River Taw. It was renamed Barnstaple Town in 1886 and replaced by a new station, 250 yards to the west, in 1898. This new facility also accommodated the Lynton & Barnstaple Railway. On 15 August 1968 D812 *Royal Naval Reserve 1859-1959* can be glimpsed entering with the 1055 Ilfracombe to Exeter St David's train. A loop had been located on the left, but this was removed in 1964.

The signal box is still standing in July 2005, although literally overshadowed by housing. Behind it the station building with its canopy also survives, occupied by a special school. *R. A. Lumber/DHM*

BRAUNTON: Class 42 No D817 *Foxhound* enters with the 1820 Ilfracombe to Exeter St David's train on Saturday 27 July 1968; this was the return working of stock used on the through train from Paddington. It is passing the signal box that had been reduced to a ground frame in the previous December when the down line had been taken out of use. The station nameboard includes 'For Saunton Sands and Croyde Bay', referring to nearby seaside attractions.

The main station building is to the left of the camera in both views, and is now occupied as a shop. The buildings on both sides of the pictures link the 'past' and 'present' scenes. *R. A. Lumber/DHM*

MORTEHOE & WOOLACOMBE station was located near Turnpike Cross, with both named places actually on the coast, 2 miles to the west. 'Battle of Britain' 4-6-2 No 34065 *Hurricane* arrives with the 4.50pm Ilfracombe to Exeter Central train on 14 September 1963. The distant road bridge marks the summit of the line.

After the line's closure the station escaped demolition, with the station house occupied privately. From 1987 a children's theme park, 'Once Upon a Time', was developed. The platforms survive, with play equipment now located between them. The bridge has been removed and the road widened. *John Scrace/DHM*

ILFRACOMBE: From Mortehoe the line descended all the way to the terminus for about 3 miles, much at a gradient of 1 in 36. Despite this steep approach, the station was still perched on the hillside overlooking the town, some 225 feet above sea level. Bulleid 'Pacific' No 34072 *257 Squadron* is waiting to depart from the island platform with the 10.00am to Waterloo on 15 September 1963. The goods shed is on the right, while the coach visible on the left is standing in one of seven carriage sidings.

The line from Barnstaple closed on 3 October 1970 and a large factory and warehousing now covers the site of the station. The 2005 photo was taken from a footpath and cycleway that follows the trackbed to the south. *John Scrace/DHM*

Lynton & Barnstaple Railway

BARNSTAPLE TOWN: The 1ft 11½in gauge Lynton & Barnstaple Railway was promoted locally and opened on 16 May 1898. As previously mentioned, Barnstaple Town was a joint station with the LSWR, the narrow gauge line occupying a bay on one side of the single platform. Manning Wardle 2-6-2T No 761 *Taw* awaits departure in the 1930s. This was one of three such locos built for the line's opening.

This area is now occupied by flats and car parking, but the end of the main station building can still be seen. The terrace of buildings on the left survives but is now largely hidden by trees. *Collection of J. W. Armstrong Trust/DHM*

CHELFHAM station was built on a hillside in a delightful and isolated location with a minimal local population. It was a passing point, which on the occasion of this photograph was being visited by a single-coach train. It is thought to be possibly an officer's 'jolly', and is believed to have been taken in about 1935, shortly before the line closed. Behind the camera is a 112-yard-long viaduct built of brick on masonry piers, which was the major engineering feature on the line.

The station is now owned by the revived Lynton & Barnstaple Railway and is used as accommodation for volunteers. The listed viaduct still dominates its secluded valley. *Collection of J. W. Armstrong Trust/DHM*

BLACKMOOR was the principal passing point and was situated at a crossroads, 900 feet above sea level and also remote from much habitation. The station buildings were constructed in a Swiss chalet style, similar to those at Woody Bay and Lynton. Pictured on a wet day in 1927, a train bound for Barnstaple awaits the arrival of a down working. The railway always struggled financially and its sale to the Southern Railway was completed in March 1923.

The main station building has been extended and now forms part of 'The Old Station House Inn'. The 'new' railway hopes to run to the right of this site. *E. S. Youldon collection/DHM*

WOODY BAY: Located at Martinhoe Cross and originally named Wooda Bay, it was intended that this station should serve a planned holiday resort several miles to the north. This development failed to materialise, but a substantial hotel was built adjacent to the station. On the extreme right, a lengthy Lynton-bound train awaits departure; it is possibly Sunday 29 September 1935, when the last train before closure was a special excursion comprising nine packed coaches hauled by Nos 188 *Lew* and 759 *Yeo*.

This is now the headquarters for the revived railway, which has thus far re-instated track for half a mile towards the site of Parracombe Halt. During the summer of 2005 loaned Hudswell Clarke 0-6-0WT *Bronllwyd* was working on Sundays, and is seen here on the far end of the coaches. On the right is a Simplex diesel named *Holwell Castle*, which operated on other days. *Collection of J. W. Armstrong Trust/DHM*

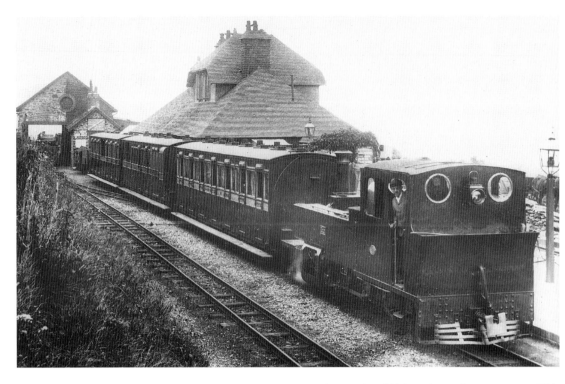

LYNTON: The terminus of the 19½-mile line was remote from, and more than 200 feet above, the town centre. This was largely due to opposition from local landowners when the line was built. Another of the original Manning Wardle tanks, *Exe*, is pictured prior to departure from the main platform in pre-SR days. The bay platform is just visible on the right, while the goods shed and office are behind the train.

Both the station house and former goods shed are now occupied as dwellings. All of the 'present' pictures on this line were taken on 10 July 2005. *E. S. Youldon collection/DHM*

Barnstaple Junction to Hole

BARNSTAPLE JUNCTION: The line to a new dock at Fremington was opened in 1848 as a standard gauge horse-worked railway. It was later converted to broad gauge and passenger services commenced in August 1854; an extension to Bideford opened in the following year. It was leased to the LSWR in 1862 and, following the addition of a third rail, standard gauge trains began running in March 1863. Ivatt 2-6-2T No 41216 is pictured arriving with the 2.15pm from Torrington on 30 September 1963. The gated private siding on the right was used by several different companies over the years.

The same view in July 2005 shows a construction site. *R. A. Lumber/DHM*

FREMINGTON: From Barnstaple the railway followed the south bank of the River Taw. This station was located just to the east of Fremington Pill (a creek), and adjacent to the quay, which was built because of difficulties in navigating the river to Barnstaple. The village is three-quarters of a mile away on the other side of the Pill. The original platform is on the right, while the tall signal box is standing on the later up platform. The building on the left is on the quayside, where the main commodities handled were imported coal, including that used by the LSWR for its locos, with ball clay from Marland and Meeth as the main export.

The signal box was closed in November 1968 when the loop was taken out of use, and the quay closed at the end of 1969. The overgrown up platform is seen on a glorious evening in July 2005, but the 'Tarka Trail' has replaced the track. A visitor centre and café are on the right. *E. S. Youldon collection/DHM*

INSTOW village looks out over the Torridge Estuary with Appledore on the opposite bank. On an appropriately damp and dismal 6 November 1982, No 31174 approaches the village with BR's 'The Last Atlantic Coast Express' excursion, the final public train to Torrington. It is just about to pass under a bridge that, until bypassed, had carried the main Barnstaple to Bideford A39 road. No 31158 is at the rear of 15 coaches carrying 843 passengers, without doubt the longest and best patronised train ever to traverse these rails.

To the left of the train is an area of sand dunes that would not have held any great appeal on that day, but which were teeming with sun worshippers in August 2005. This section of the 'Tarka Trail' also forms part of the South West Peninsular Coast Path. *Both DHM*

INSTOW: BR Sulzer-engined Type 2 No 25225 approaches the station on 6 October 1978 with the 0830 daily trip working from Barnstaple Junction, comprising ten loaded fertiliser vans for Torrington and 20 empty clay wagons for Marland and Meeth. Visible above the rear cab of the 'Rat' is the chimney belonging to the 13-lever signal box. This had been a busy box in passenger train days, as this was the main crossing point between Barnstaple and Torrington, and the signalman also had to deal with the A39 level crossing.

The loop had been taken out of use in November 1968, and after the road was bypassed the crossing was equipped with automatic lights and the box closed on 17 January 1979. It survived demolition, however, and is looked after by the Bideford & Instow Railway Group. Rails are still embedded in the road and a short stretch of track runs in front of it. Replica crossing gates have been installed and the interior restored. *Both DHM*

BIDEFORD: This ancient port was the largest town served by the line. The station opened in 1872 when it replaced the original broad gauge facility, which then became a goods station. The new station was built in a district known as East-the-Water, the town centre being reached via the adjacent Bideford Bridge. Also across the Torridge, the Bideford, Westward Ho! & Appledore Railway operated from 1901 to 1917. 'M7' No 30255 waits with a Torrington train on 17 August 1951; the signal box is just out of view on the left.

Devon County Council now owns the site and uses the main building. The 'Tarka Trail' runs through the station, but the Bideford & Instow Group have rebuilt the signal box, the original having been demolished, and re-laid some track. The Mark 1 coach is used as a café. Behind the camera is a short stretch of running track where a Planet diesel occasionally operates. *R. A. Lumber/DHM*

TORRINGTON: The LSWR opened an extension to here in July 1872. The station was rather inconveniently sited on the side of the Torridge valley, with the market town of Great Torrington a mile away and 200 feet higher up the hillside. Its status as a terminus changed in 1925 when the North Devon & Cornwall Junction Light Railway opened between here and Halwill Junction. The new line was operated by the Southern Railway, although technically an independent company until nationalisation in 1948. The two lines were worked as separate systems connecting here, and trains did not normally work through. Ex-LBSCR Class 'E1/R' No 2608 waits to depart with a Barnstaple train in May 1935.

A short section of track beside the 'Tarka Trail' provides a memorial to the railway in 2005. *Author's collection/DHM*

TORRINGTON: Milk was an important source of revenue for the railway. A large Unigate creamery was located in Torrington and milk was delivered to the station by lorry and pumped into the stainless steel tank wagons. Class 22 No D6334 stands with the 1645 milk train to Exeter on 9 October 1968. The milk loading facility was located at the end of the siding through the goods shed, and the pipework could only handle three tank wagons at a time, which meant that a good deal of shunting could be required to prepare a train. A milk lorry is standing next to the shed, and just above it can be noted the short tunnel for the long closed Torrington & Marland Railway.

A fertiliser warehouse was opened in 1976 on the site of the goods shed, and today it is occupied by a transport company, with a cycle hire business on the far side. This lower angle was selected in preference to showing a close-up of trees! *R. A. Lumber/DHM*

TORRINGTON: Viewed from the road bridge that leads to the town, Ivatt Prairie tank No 41283 is about to leave with the 4.00pm to Halwill on 30 September 1963. The steam in the background is from sister engine No 41224 engaged in shunting after arriving with the 3.18pm from Barnstaple Junction.

A new milk loading depot was opened on the up platform in March 1976. The pipework could now deal with seven wagons at a time and was protected by a canopy. On 6 October 1978 milk is being pumped from lorries into rail tankers; that afternoon nine were taken to Barnstaple by No 25225. Despite this busy scene, this traffic was soon to be lost to rail, with the final milk train leaving here just six days later.

Passenger services to Halwill were withdrawn from 1 March 1965, those to Barnstaple continuing until 2 October that year. Freight traffic ensured the route's survival as far as Meeth until 1982, latterly operating as a siding from Barnstaple. Devon County Council subsequently acquired the trackbed, and the section from Barnstaple to beyond Petrockstow now forms part of the 'Tarka Trail' footpath and cycleway, completed in 1992. The main station building here is now the 'Puffing Billy' public house, and a clay wagon and brake-van remind visitors of the area's history. *R. A. Lumber/DHM (2)*

Below Looking back to 11 May 1950, 'M7' No 250 is still in Southern livery as it arrives with a train from Barnstaple. A turntable had been located to the left, but was removed by 1930 as most services were being operated by tank engines. An engine shed was also located here, but closed in 1959 with its engines and drivers transferred to its parent depot at Barnstaple Junction. *J. H. Bamsey*

TORRINGTON VIADUCT: The Torrington & Marland Railway was a 3-foot-gauge mineral line that opened in January 1881, and was built primarily to serve the clay and brick works at Marland. The line commenced at an interchange siding in Torrington goods yard, then passed through the aforementioned tunnel under the main road. Shortly afterwards it crossed the River Torridge on a timber viaduct. When the ND&CLR replaced its narrow gauge predecessor, a steel viaduct on masonry piers was erected alongside the original structure. No 33119 is passing over this viaduct on 25 June 1978 as it returns with the 1610 Meeth to Paddington railtour.
Today the viaduct forms part of the 'Tarka Trail'. *Both DHM*

TORRINGTON VIADUCT: In an unusual view taken on the viaduct, the same RPPR 'Devon Quarryman' charter is pictured on its outward journey after previously visiting Meldon Quarry. Starting from Paddington at 0752, here No 33119 is tailing 33103 and 4TC sets Nos 418 and 420 as the train crawls over the bridge at a maximum of 10mph. The wooden viaduct had stood to the left of its replacement. *J. R. Norgrove/DHM*

WATERGATE HALT: The ND&CLR followed much of the route of the narrow gauge line for its first 6 miles, but with some deviations to ease gradients and curves. After leaving the Torridge valley it climbed up another valley before arriving at Watergate Bridge, where the B3227 road from Torrington to Holsworthy crossed the railway via an ungated crossing. Ivatt tanks Nos 41206 and 41291 wait with the RCTS/PRC 'Exmoor Ranger' special at 1.00pm on Saturday 27 March 1965. A siding had been located on the right, but this had closed in May 1960 and was lifted shortly afterwards.

Car parking is now provided here for those wishing to use the trail. *R. A. Lumber/DHM*

WATERGATE HALT: The two tank engines have eased over the road at the permitted speed of 5mph and are now passing the halt, which is just visible in front of the leading loco. Passenger services from Torrington to Halwill had ended exactly one month earlier, with the line south from Meeth clay works closing completely. However, the track was kept intact until this train had run. With a 10.12am departure time from Exeter St David's, the special later visited Ilfracombe and also traversed the Barnstaple to Taunton line.

The simple halt was of concrete construction and opened on 20 September 1926, a year after the line. Long enough for a single coach, no shelter was provided for its regular customers, which prior to the motor car era were a few men travelling to and from their labours at Marland works. In later years any use was minimal.

Today the formation is shrouded by trees, but the overgrown platform survives next to the trail. *R. A. Lumber/E. S. Youldon collection/ DHM*

YARDE HALT: The line continued to climb at 1 in 45 towards the summit, about 450 feet above sea level and about half a mile north of this halt. To reach the summit, the ND&CJLR deviated from the original narrow gauge alignment and traversed some of the heaviest earthworks on the route, required to ease the steep gradients. The halt opened on 19 July 1926 to serve the small community of East Yarde, which mainly comprised a long row of cottages built by the North Devon Clay Company for its workers. The halt had, however, seen its last passenger when photographed in August 1968.

The platform is another survivor in 2005; the cottages are to the right of the camera. *Bernard Mills/DHM*

DUNSBEAR HALT: After cresting the summit, the line descended at up to 1 in 50 for over a mile before reaching this halt. Opening with the line, at one time this was the busiest station south of Torrington, when it was used by about 70 clay workers each day; the Marland works was a walk of less than a mile away. Ivatt 2MT No 41312 pauses with the single-coach 8.52am Torrington to Halwill service on 25 September 1962. Until 1960 a siding had existed on the left of the train. Immediately after leaving, the train will pass over another ungated crossing. Although somewhat overgrown, this platform also still stands next to the Trail. *R. C. Riley/DHM*

MARLAND SIDING: The ball clay works here and at Meeth were the main reason for the construction of the ND&CJLR. Until 1970 Marland works had its own 3-foot-gauge railway, from which clay was transhipped into standard gauge wagons. On 18 August 1978 No 25225 failed here with the daily clay train. No 25223 was sent light engine from Exeter on a rescue mission and is now pulling the errant loco and loaded train out of the siding.

By 1982 this traffic was all that remained on the line, but with a need to replace the worn-out wagon fleet and also upgrade the track, BR decided that there was insufficient business to justify the expenditure and the last clay trains ran in September that year. The entrance to the siding is now heavily overgrown, but the gate post survives to mark the spot in 2005. *Both DHM*

PETROCKSTOW: Its namesake village (actually spelled with a final 'e') is just over half a mile to the south-west. The station had two platforms, a crossing loop and a two-siding goods yard. The engineer for the ND&CJLR was the famous Col H. F. Stephens, who managed a number of independent light railways in Britain. As was normal with such railways, all the crossings on the line were ungated and there were no signal boxes, all loops and sidings being controlled from ground frames. However, this also meant that there was a maximum line speed of 25mph. No 41313 is passing over another crossing as it arrives with a Torrington to Halwill train, typically comprising a single coach.

Another car park for the 'Tarka Trail' is to the left, and the trail itself now runs along the former up platform before regaining the trackbed at the south end of the station site. *John Smith, Terry Gough collection/DHM*

HOLE station, another crossing place, could be found in a remote spot down a track, half a mile south of the A3072 at Windmilland Cross. The nameboard included 'For Black Torrington', referring to a village more than a mile to the north, and it is assumed that the station was not so named to avoid confusion with Torrington. Hole is a tiny hamlet several miles to the west! No 41223 is departing with the 10.40am Halwill to Torrington train on 29 August 1964, the penultimate Saturday of steam working. The train actually started at Hole that day due to a token failure between Halwill and here, the one or two passengers having been brought from Halwill by taxi.

The station is now a dwelling. To the east a section of the formation is used as part of a footpath to the village of Highampton. *Bernard Mills/DHM*

Coleford Junction to Meldon Junction

COLEFORD JUNCTION was created when the standard gauge Devon & Cornwall Railway opened as far as North Tawton on 1 November 1865; the new route diverged sharply to the left of the Barnstaple line on a 20-chain curve. A pair of 'Bubble cars' head away from the junction forming the 1530 Exeter to Okehampton service on Saturday 4 July 1970. The 13-lever signal box is hidden by the tree on the extreme right of the picture, while its up inner home signal is on the left.

The box closed on 17 October 1971, since when the two routes have operated independently from Crediton. On 24 May 1997 No 37667 *Meldon Quarry Centenary 1897-1997* is tailing No 37415 on the 1720 Meldon to Exeter St David's train, which was one of two return trips carrying invited guests prior to the Sunday DMU service commencing on the following day. The loco had been named earlier at Okehampton. *R. A. Lumber/DHM*

NORTH TAWTON station was located more than a mile south of the town. A solitary passenger is depicted as Type 2 diesel-hydraulic No D6342 arrives with a Plymouth to Exeter train on 25 July 1964. It is passing the 18-lever platform-mounted signal box, and to the right is a sizeable goods shed. A minor road runs beneath the platform behind the camera.

The goods yard closed in June 1965 and the signal box suffered a similar fate in September 1967. The line was singled in October 1971 and the residual passenger service to Okehampton ceased in June 1972. In the second view, also from the station footbridge, 'Peak' No 45022 is passing the boarded-up station on 22 March 1982 with the 7B54 1500 Meldon Quarry to Bristol East Depot ballast train.

The third photograph was taken a little to the east on 28 May 1984, and shows No 31259 returning from Meldon with a portion of 'The Devonian' railtour. Originating in Preston, the train had split in Exeter, with the other part going forward to Paignton behind a pair of Class 40s. The footbridge has been removed for re-erection at Ropley on the Mid Hants Railway, the minor road is being upgraded, and to cater for large lorries the old overbridge is to be replaced, with the track raised by several feet to give greater headroom. A section of the down platform has been removed as part of this work.

As seen in the final picture the track is now above platform level. 'Skipper' DMUs Nos 142019/023 pass with the 1035 Okehampton to Exeter Central 'Dartmoor Rambler' service on 16 August 1986. West Devon Borough Council sponsored two return trips on each of four Saturdays that summer. *R. C. Riley/DHM(3)*

SAMPFORD COURTENAY: The Devon & Cornwall Railway opened an extension to a new terminus, known as Okehampton Road, on 8 January 1867. When trains started running to Okehampton itself in October 1871, the station was renamed Belstone Corner, after its actual location. However, less than three months later it was named after a village more than a mile to the north. The Crediton to Okehampton road crosses the railway here, and in a view from the bridge an Okehampton-bound 'Bubble car' is seen in July 1971.

The Dartmoor Railway has built a new platform here, long enough for about three coaches. On Sunday 17 July 2005 No 150236 departs as the 0906 Exeter Central to Okehampton service. *Bernard Mills/DHM*

AMPFORD COURTENAY: Despite its original terminus status, the station was only provided with a modest single-
storey main building on the up side, which incorporated the booking office and hall, waiting room and toilets.
No living accommodation was provided in this building, but there was housing provided nearby for railway staff.
A waiting shelter stood on the down platform, but there was never a connecting footbridge – passengers had to
use either the road bridge or a barrow crossing.

The derelict building provides a sad sight on 23 March 1982 as 'Crompton' No 33028 passes with the 6V80 0535
Salisbury to Meldon empties, and was demolished later in the decade. *E. S. Youldon collection/DHM*

SAMPFORD COURTENAY: On 16 May 1964 a 'Hymek' diesel failed while working the 1.00pm Waterloo t
Plymouth train, so Standard 5MT 4-6-0 No 73074 was taken off an up freight and pressed into use from Yeofore
The duo are pictured at 6.50pm, more than an hour late. The goods yard on the left had closed in April 1961, wit
the track removed by November 1963. The small wooden goods shed and adjacent slaughterhouse were sti
standing at this time.

A joinery company now occupies the site of the goods yard. The concrete platelayers' hut survives today an
provides a link with the past. *R. A. Lumber/DHM*

OKEHAMPTON: A small wooden engine shed was provided here in 1894, and extended to provide additional accommodation in 1914. It was, however, destroyed by fire in 1920, damaging two locos inside, and was replaced by a new concrete building at a cost of £1,500. It was a sub-shed to Exmouth Junction and did not normally have an allocation of locomotives. In BR days three or four engines were often stabled overnight, usually from the 'N' and 'T9' Classes. The shed was scheduled to close on 1 January 1965, but remained open until the following June. 6-4T No 80041 is pictured on 27 March that year.
  The building was subsequently demolished and a car park now covers the site. *Author's collection/DHM*

OKEHAMPTON: This fine panorama of the east end of the station from 2 January 1965 includes the new order i the form of Class 42 No D815 *Druid*, which is waiting with a Plymouth to Brighton train. Its steam heating boiler working well on this crisp winter's day, while on the right steam is largely obscuring Standard 4MT 4-6-0 No 7502: In front of it is the 70-foot turntable that replaced a smaller version in 1947, and was thus able to handle large engines such as the 'S15' 4-6-0s that could now be used on Meldon ballast trains. Also clearly visible are the good shed on the left and the large water tower next to the 'Warship'. The engine shed is just out of view on the right.

An unusually busy scene from 18 September 1971 includes Birmingham RC&W Co Nos W51328 and W513 after arrival as the 1736 service from Exeter St David's. On the right Brush Type 4 No 1823 (later 47342) has ru round its empty stock after working the 1Z18 1326 North Camp (Aldershot) to Okehampton military special.

After the passenger service from Exeter was withdrawn from 5 June 1972, some goods continued to be handled for a few years, mainly fertiliser and military traffic. The line was, however, primarily retained for ballast trains from Meldon Quarry. Surprisingly the station evaded demolition and remained substantially intact for more than 30 years, even receiving the occasional special passenger working. The third photograph shows No 33028 passing the slowly decaying structures with the 1500 train from Meldon to Bristol East Depot on 23 March 1982.

Finally, the July 2005 view was taken a little further forward due to the presence of a building on the right that houses a cycle hire business. *Peter W. Gray/DHM(3)*

OKEHAMPTON: The station saw its first trains for public use on 3 October 1871, but most of the structures visib⌐
in these 'past' views date from 1930-32 when it was modernised. One of Dugald Drummond's graceful 'T9's, ℸ
30712, waits in Platform 1 on 15 September 1951. This bay platform was normally used by trains starting fro⌐
here and bound for either the Bude or North Cornwall lines. The substantial goods shed is on the right, wℸ
station pilot No 30581 also just visible.

The goods shed is now occupied as the Youth Hostels Association's 'Okehampton Adventure Centre'. DEMU ℸ
205032 is departing for Meldon on 9 August 2005 after completing its duties for the day. *J. H. Bamsey/DHM*

OKEHAMPTON: The original signal box was on the down platform, but was replaced in 1936 by a new brick structure positioned at the west end of the up platform. Containing a 35-lever frame, its foundation walls at the rear were built on an embankment, as the land falls away steeply at this point. 'Greyhound' No 30709 is arriving with the 3.13pm Padstow to Exeter Central train on 8 April 1960.

The box closed in July 1972, and was used as an office for a period. After its closure, only one train was allowed in the section from Crediton to Meldon. The Dartmoor Railway has, however, introduced an additional staff-operated section from here to Meldon. Freightliner's No 66507 approaches with the 6F95 1030 Meldon Quarry to Tinksey Yard ballast train on 12 July 2005. *R. A. Lumber/DHM*

OKEHAMPTON: Up trains used Platform 3, and if they were terminating services from Bude or Padstow it wa usual for the station pilot to couple to the rear of the train and shunt it to the bay platform ready for the ne departure to the west. This possible scenario was recorded on 15 September 1951 as Adams '0395' Class 0-6-0 N 30581 stands beneath the station footbridge. An engine from this class had often been used as resident pilot her since LSWR days. This particular loco dated from 1885 and was withdrawn in March 1953.

The former up rails were retained as the main running line when the route was singled in 1971, the down ma being kept as a siding. In another view from the 'wilderness years', No 50042 *Triumph* trundles through with th 7C38 11.40 Exeter Riverside to Meldon ballast empties on 23 August 1988.

In the third view Nos 37308 and 37047 pass through the restored station with the 6G94 0850 St Blazey to Meldo empties on 4 February 2004. DMU 150242 is unusually parked on the right as Wessex Trains was using th Dartmoor Railway for new driver training at this time. *J. H. Bamsey/author's collection/DHM*

NEAR OKEHAMPTON: The station was built on a level section, but thereafter the line continued its 1 in 77 climb beside Dartmoor. Pictured from Park Road Bridge 'T9' No 30716 is making a spirited departure with a North Cornwall service in July 1950. The moor has long been used by the Army for training, and the Military Sidings and loading platform can be glimpsed on the left; these dated from the 1890s.

The Surbiton to Okehampton car carrier trains were also loaded and unloaded in these sidings from 1960 to 1964 but they were taken out of use in 1982. EWS No 66052 passes with the 6F94 1241 Par to Meldon ballast empties on 31 August 2004. Access to the 'Granite Way' is gained immediately below this field of view. *J. H. Bamsey/DHM*

NEAR OKEHAMPTON: 'N' Class 2-6-0 No 31859 descends towards Okehampton with a freight from Halwill Junction (and beyond) at 7.35pm on 4 August 1964. Many of the wagons are loaded with ball clay from the Meeth and Marland area. To the right of the tracks is a footpath to Meldon Quarry that was used by both quarry workers and railway staff; the quarry is more than a mile to the west.

'Thumper' DEMU No 205032 slowly descends forming the 1700 Meldon Viaduct to Okehampton service on 9 August 2005. On the right is the 'Granite Way', a section of National Cycle Network Route 27 that runs from Ilfracombe to Plymouth. *Peter W. Gray/DHM*

MELDON QUARRY: Industrial activity in the area pre-dated the arrival of the railway, and in 1886 a siding was opened to serve a small privately owned quarry. During construction of the line, the civil engineer determined that the local hornfels rock would make excellent track ballast. Despite its remoteness from much of its network, the LSWR purchased the quarry in 1897 and soon set about expanding operations by installing new machinery and additional sidings. In a panorama from the top of the quarry face on 19 July 1958 we can see a Bulleid 'Pacific' just about to pass the signal box with an up train. The engine shed is in the centre of the picture with the loading plant to its right.

A similar viewpoint was recorded on 17 June 1992, during an evening visit by the RCTS West of England branch, and shows the developments that had taken place in the intervening years. A part of the engine shed can be glimpsed beyond the modern plant on the right, with quarry shunter No 08945 standing outside.

Hugh Davies /DHM

MELDON QUARRY: A tiny halt was constructed in the 1920s from standard components manufactured at Exmout Junction concrete works. It was provided for the exclusive use of quarry and railway staff and their families, cottages having been built adjacent to the quarry for workers. The platforms were only long enough for on coach. No 34023 *Blackmore Vale* is passing with a train from Plymouth on 19 July 1958.

The halt was probably demolished in the 1960s. A temporary platform was erected in 1997 for an event on 2 May celebrating both the centenary of the quarry and the re-opening of Okehampton station. No 37415 is on th rear of the 1004 train from Exeter, which is obscuring this platform. *Hugh Davies/DHM*

MELDON QUARRY: Pictured from near the site of the halt on 3 June 1972 are the signal box, concrete loading screens and the engine shed housing shunter No 3525 (later 08410). The brick-built box had replaced an earlier cabin, but had itself been closed in March 1970. The screens were obsolete by this time, replaced by more modern equipment on the right. The concrete engine shed had replaced a wooden structure in the 1950s.

The Dartmoor Railway has opened a station here, known as Meldon Viaduct, and advertises it as the highest in southern England. A view from its platform on 4 February 2004 includes No 47716 stabled on the left and Nos 37308 and 37047 as they run round after arriving with ballast empties from St Blazey. When the track layout was modified in about 1990, the west end of the shed was blocked up and the far end opened up instead. *Both DHM*

107

MELDON VIADUCT: Shortly after leaving the quarry, the line continues its 1 in 77 climb and crosses the valley of the River Okement on this slender 150-foot-high structure, built of steel on stone plinths, on a right-hand curve of 30 chains radius. On 27 April 1963 No 34081 *92 Squadron* is rumbling over at a maximum of 20mph with the Plymouth portion of the 9.00am from Waterloo.

In the 1960s the maintenance costs for this viaduct were cited as a factor when determining the future of the route. The up line was taken out of use in April 1966, but even after the line closed in 1968 the only access to the quarry sidings for a further two years was from track on the viaduct; and a head shunt was retained on it until 1990. Today the 'Granite Way' passes over and offers spectacular views. *Derek Frost/DHM*

ELDON JUNCTION: The line from Okehampton to Lydford opened in October 1874, but the signal box did not pen until 11 May 1878 when a loop was provided on the single-track line. Known as Meldon Loop, it was named in 1879 when the line to Holsworthy opened, and the track was doubled between Meldon Quarry and ydford later the same year. Located at a remote spot some 900 feet above sea level, this was the highest box on e Southern Railway standard gauge network.

The box closed in 1968, and there is no hint of its existence in 2005 as cyclists head westward. *Bernard ills/DHM*

MELDON JUNCTION: The roof of the signal box can just be seen above the first coach as 'West Country' No 3402
Seaton forges past the junction with the 1130am Brighton to Plymouth train in September 1963. The Nort
Cornwall line trails in on the left; the facing crossover had replaced a double-track junction in the previou
December. Just visible in the background are two cottages provided for the signalmen.

The 'Granite Way' now follows the Plymouth line and some wooden seating is provided at the site of th
junction. Behind the camera the route of the North Cornwall line is steadily becoming overgrown. *Berna.
Mills/DHM*

Routes to North Cornwall

MADDAFORD MOOR HALT was actually located at the hamlet of Thorndon Cross, just over 2 miles from Meldon Junction, and opened on 27 July 1926. It was built on the site of a passing loop and signal box that had been in use from 1899 to 1921, and its purpose was to serve a proposed health resort; however, little came of this, although some housing development in the area did provide custom for the railway. The simple concrete structure is pictured in the summer of 1967, the line having closed in the previous October.

The site is heavily overgrown in 2005 with no obvious evidence of the halt's existence. *Terry Gough/DHM*

ASHBURY (FOR NORTHLEW): Opening with the line, this station was set in a sparsely populated area, but act[e] as a railhead for a number of villages, including the one named in the suffix, and which was more than 2 mil[to the north. It was the only passing place between Meldon and Halwill after the Maddaford Moor loop close[d]. Its quiet existence is, however, coming to an end on 3 September 1966 as two 'Bubble cars' call forming the 11.[Okehampton to Bude service – the line will be closed exactly one month later. The 1879-vintage signal box ca[n be noted on the up platform.

The station is now occupied as a dwelling. *R. A. Lumber/DHM*

ALWILL JUNCTION: When the Devon & Cornwall Railway opened to Holsworthy in January 1879, 'Halwill & ...eaworthy' station was provided to serve the two hamlets, being situated about halfway between them. It grew ... importance when the North Cornwall line opened to Launceston and was renamed to match its new status. By ...e time the ND&CJLR to Torrington opened in 1925, the signal box was holding four separate tablet machines ...r the four converging single-line routes. 'N' Class 2-6-0 No 31845 is leaving with the up Bude goods at 6.05pm ...n 22 August 1964, two weeks before such services ended. Beyond the brake van, 2-6-2T No 41249 is arriving with ...Torrington train.

The village retains its railway name in 2005, but housing has been built on the site of the station, served by ...ads named 'Beeching Close' and 'Stationfields'. The house just visible to the immediate right of the 'N' can also ... seen in July 2005. *Peter W. Gray/DHM*

DUNSLAND CROSS station was located in a remote area half a mile south of the crossroads of that name and almost 500 feet above sea level. There was no obvious reason for its existence, but the station nameboard also advised 'Alight here for Shebbear College', referring to a boys' public school several miles away. Standard 3MT 2-6-2T No 82017 pauses with the 1.55pm Bude to Okehampton train on 5 July 1961 before commencing a 1 in climb to Halwill. The signal box contained an 11-lever frame, but the tablet instruments were unusually sited the booking office, which is out of sight on the left.

The box closed on 2 January 1966 when all track was taken out of use other than the down platform loop, which was retained for the remaining DMU service. Today the formation has been grassed over and the 'present' view includes the main station building, which is now a dwelling. The goods shed (to the left) has been converted into holiday accommodation and an archery centre has also been established here. *Terry Gough/DHM*

HOLSWORTHY: The terminus of the Devon & Cornwall Railway served an important market town. A slaughterhouse was established here and much meat and livestock traffic was handled by the railway. Five cattle pens were provided on a siding that could hold five wagons, and on a busy day several dozen such wagons would be loaded; this siding can be noted on the left as 'N' No 31837 waits with the 1.18pm Okehampton to Bude train on 5 July 1961. The original platform is on the left; the down one was added when the line was extended to Bude.

The once substantial freight business was largely lost to road competition through the 1950s, and the final goods trains serving West Devon and North Cornwall operated on 5 September 1964. After total closure, the main station buildings survived in commercial use, but in recent years they were demolished to make way for a supermarket. The terrace of houses on the right are the best comparison points in 2005. *Terry Gough/DHM*

WHITSTONE & BRIDGERULE: The LSWR opened the extension to Bude on 10 August 1898, but work on this, th[e] only intermediate station, was not complete then, and it did not open until 1 November. The railway crossed th[e] Tamar shortly before entering this station, and although this river marks much of the boundary between Devo[n] and Cornwall, hereabouts a small area of the former juts into the Royal Duchy, and the branch will actually cro[ss] the border about a mile to the west. 'T9' No 30715 stands with what is probably the 1.18pm Okehampton to Bud[e] train, the regular 'Greyhound' duty on this line, on 23 August 1960.

The line closed on 3 October 1966 and today the station is occupied as a private residence, with the formatio[n] filled to platform level. The minor road bridge survives to identify the location in July 2005. *R. A. Lumber/DHM*

ASHWATER: The LSWR was involved in promoting the North Cornwall Railway, with the first section from Halwill to Launceston opening on 21 July 1886. The first station on the line was 5 miles from Halwill and actually located at the hamlet of Ashmill in the narrow valley of the River Carey, with the larger Ashwater about half a mile to the west. It is seen from a very narrow road bridge on 22 August 1964. The main buildings were on the up side, with the signal box and a waiting shelter on the opposite platform. The goods yard is on the right.

The yard was to close in a couple of weeks and the station became an unstaffed halt on 7 November 1965, the signal box also closing that day. The road bridge survives in 2005, but the same view today is heavily wooded and meaningless. It was bypassed when the road was straightened, with an embankment built to carry it between the bridge and the main station building. The latter is now a dwelling and is seen from its approach road in July 2005. A coal merchant occupies the site of the goods yard. *Peter W. Gray/DHM*

TOWER HILL: The next station on the line was more than 3 miles from Ashwater and was of an identical ston construction. In a remote spot in this thinly populated area, it was named after an adjacent farm. Originally crossing place, the signal box closed in 1920, thus creating a 7-mile section from Ashwater to Launceston. In 194 the down loop was restored, the goods yard expanded and a signal box established in the booking hall, all t serve nearby US ammunition dumps. After this short-lived activity, the station remained a useful crossing plac as illustrated on 29 August 1960; 'T9' No 30709 waits with the 9.56am Okehampton to Padstow train as 'Battle Britain' No 34069 *Hawkinge* passes with the 8.30am 'Atlantic Coast Express' from Padstow.

This line also closed on 3 October 1966 and the station was subsequently demolished. The land is occupied a paddocks and smallholdings by the owners of a row of former railway cottages that stand to the left. A roa bridge can be glimpsed in the right background of the 'past' view and this survives today. *R. A. Lumber/DHM*

Bridestowe to Tavistock North

BRIDESTOWE: The LSWR opened its line from Okehampton to Lydford in 1874. From Meldon Junction it continued to climb around the northern boundary of Dartmoor for about half a mile before reaching its summit, then started a 13-mile descent towards Tavistock. This station was built on a long curve, with the village almost miles to the north. From about 1880 to the late 1920s a horse-drawn 7-mile-long standard gauge line ran from ere to the Rattlebrook Peat Works on Dartmoor. In this undated view, a 'T9' in original condition is arriving with down stopper while an up goods shunts the yard, which runs to the left behind the signal box. The peat railway iding is at the far end of the down platform.

The station is now a private residence, and although the trackbed has been in-filled to platform level, many eatures survive, including the footbridge from which the previous picture was taken. It is seen in August 2005 rom the adjacent road bridge. *Author's collection/DHM*

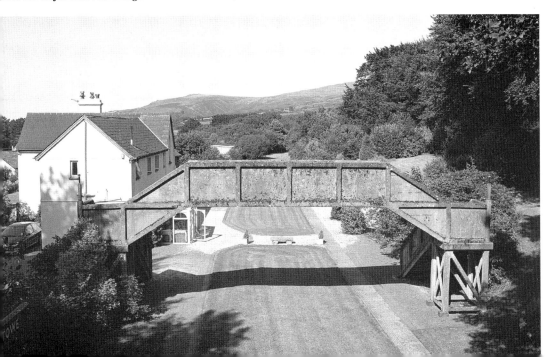

LYDFORD: The broad gauge Launceston & South Devon Railway opened in 1865. It followed the valley of the River Lyd to the west from here, and although its station was close to the beautiful Lydford Gorge, it was in remote spot, with the village more than a mile to the north. When the LSWR arrived in 1874, it elected to buil its terminus adjacent to the existing station, despite its route passing close to the village. Although this was usefu for through passengers, neither railway was convenient for the local inhabitants. From 1876 LSWR trains wer able to use the broad gauge line to Plymouth after a third rail was added. On 27 April 1968 the 1638 Plymouth t Exeter DMU is depicted from Station Road bridge as it departs. Note the distinctive up advanced starting signa which had two co-acting arms on separate lattice posts; the one on top of the embankment could be seen mor easily by drivers of non-stop trains.

It is still possible to stand on the bridge, but the formation is now heavily overgrown. *R. A. Lumber/DHM*

BRENTOR: On 1 June 1890 the LSWR finally opened its own double-track line to Plymouth, the initial section flanking the western side of Dartmoor on its way to Tavistock. This station was only about 1½ miles from Lydford, close to the village of North Brentor and with an excellent view of Brent Tor itself, a conical knoll of volcanic rock with a small church on its peak and an Iron Age hill fort on its northern side. A Plymouth-bound DMU is pictured from a road bridge as it calls in the spring of 1968, shortly before the line closed. The already closed ex-GWR Launceston branch can be noted on the right, with the tor just out of view, also to the right.

The station is now a delightful dwelling, the bridge has been demolished and the road widened; the view therefrom is now one of flora, so the 'present' view was taken from the garden. *Bernard Mills/DHM*

TAVISTOCK NORTH: The two lines continued to largely parallel one another for about 4 miles to Wringworth a couple of miles north of Tavistock, where the LSWR line crossed the GWR branch before entering the ancie stannary town. The station was built on the hillside on the western side of the valley of the River Tavy, and th suffix was not added to its name until after nationalisation in September 1949. Just south of the station th railway crossed a substantial stone-built viaduct, before passing under a minor road bridge. 'T9' No 7 approaches this bridge with a Plymouth train in Southern Railway days.

Passenger services between Okehampton and Bere Alston ran for the last time on Sunday 5 May 1968. Th station master's house and booking hall survive today, with housing and council offices built on much of th station site. A footpath crosses the viaduct, but this is largely obscured by branches in August 2005. *E. S. Youlde collection/DHM*

Lifton to Tavistock South

LIFTON: A broad gauge branch line was opened from Plymouth to Tavistock in 1859. A subsequent Launceston & South Devon Railway Act allowed the construction of an extension to this line, with services to Launceston commencing on 1 July 1865. The trains were operated by the South Devon Railway, all companies eventually becoming part of the Great Western. The passenger service between Plymouth and Launceston ceased on Saturday 29 December 1962, but parts of the line were retained for freight services, including the section between Lydford and Lifton, which was kept to serve the Ambrosia creamery. The station received its last steam-hauled train on 5 September 1965 when No 41283 called with a special. The creamery is to the left of this view.

The siding to the milk factory closed on 28 February 1966, and Ambrosia eventually expanded its site to take over the station area. Now owned by Premier Foods, the factory produces creamed rice, custard and the like.
A. Lumber/DHM

CORYTON: Opening with the line, in its early days this station dealt with large quantities of manganese traffic.
solitary passenger awaits the arriving 12.40pm Launceston to Plymouth service at 12.54pm on 23 June 1962, th
sunshine enhancing this picturesque rural setting. The station served several villages including its namesak
about a mile to the east, but had been reduced in status to that of an unstaffed halt in September 1959. The engi
is the now preserved 2-6-2T No 4555, from a class that monopolised branch services for about 50 years.

The station building has now been incorporated into a fine dwelling. A different angle was selected for th
August 2005 view due to tree growth. *Peter W. Gray/DHM*

LIDDATON HALT: Situated about 1½ miles east of Coryton station, this halt was opened on 4 April 1938 to serve several small communities, and was actually slightly closer to the village of Coryton than the station bearing that name! The platform was of all-wooden construction and located next to a minor road overbridge. It closed when the branch's passenger service ended, but was visited on 5 September 1965 by a Great Western Society special celebrating the centenary of the line. Starting at Exeter St David's at 12.20, and also later visiting Bude, the four-coach train was hauled by Ivatt 2-6-2T No 41283.

The bridge is still in situ, but the view today is of a smallholding complete with grazing goats. *R. A. Lumber/DHM*

LYDFORD: The signalman approaches 2-6-2T No 5541 with the single-line tablet for exchange with the crew board the 3.05pm Plymouth to Launceston train on Saturday 9 June 1962. The LSWR station was built next to t GWR one, and is to the left in this view. Originally the two stations had their own staff, but the LSWR assum full responsibility in 1914. Each company also had its own signal box, but these were closed in 1917 and replac by the one depicted here on the centre platform. Also manned by LSWR staff, there were two frames on oppos sides of the box to control the two track layouts.

The site is now privately owned and was steadily returning to nature in 2005. *R. A. Lumber/DHM*

TAVISTOCK SOUTH was the terminus of the Tavistock & South Devon Railway when it opened on 22 June 1859. The original wooden station burned down in 1887 and was rebuilt with stone walls and the only overall roof on the line, befitting its status as the most important station on the branch. Many services from Plymouth terminated here rather than running through to Launceston. The suffix was not added to the name until 26 September 1949. Another currently preserved Prairie tank, No 5572, pauses with the 5.40pm Launceston to Plymouth train on 29 August 1960. The loco is largely obscuring the 36-lever signal box.

The box closed in July 1964, with the residual goods traffic ceasing in the following September. The site today is occupied commercially. *R. A. Lumber/DHM*

INDEX OF LOCATIONS

Every time he goes to B R he cannot come home with the ... ...